GW00864333

FOR GOD SO LOVED THE WORLD THAT HE GAVE HIS ONE AND ONLY SON, THAT WHOEVER BELIEVES IN HIM SHALL NOT PERISH BUT HAVE ETERNAL LIFE.

**JOHN 3:16**

My name:

My Age:

My favorite Bible Verse:

**The Creative Bible for Children**
Illustrations by Gill Guile
Text & Concept by CPH editorial staff
Copyright © 2017 Copenhagen Publishing House
www.copenhagenpublishing.com
ISBN 978-87-92105-12-7
Printed in China

All rights reserved. No part of this book may be reproduced or utilized in any form or by any means, electronic or mechanical, including photocopying, recording, or by any information storage and retrieval system, without prior permission in writing from the Publisher.

# The Creative
# Bible
## for Children

# The Old Testament

# The New Testament

# The Old Testament

# God Makes the World (Genesis 1)

The Bible tells us that in the beginning God created the heavens and the earth. The earth was cold and dark, without any shape, life or light. Then God began to create order and beauty in the world. God said, "Let there be light!" and there was light. God saw that the light was good and He called the light "day" and the darkness He called "night."

God then started to create everything we know. In just seven days God made everything. He made the dry land and the oceans. He made the fish swimming in the seas and the birds flying in the skies.

Afterwards God made two great lights – the sun and the moon. God set them in place in the heavens to give light to the earth and to divide the light from the darkness. He also made all of the stars.

God then made the wild animals such as lions, tigers and elephants. He made the tame animals such as cattle, sheep and dogs. He saw that it was good. But something important was still missing...

Can you find the hidden star?

LET THERE BE LIGHT

"God created the world and saw that it was good."

# Adam & Eve (Genesis 2-3)

God took some dust. From it He created Adam, the first man. God put Adam in a wonderful garden called Eden. God saw it was not good for Adam to be alone, so as he slept, God took out one of Adam's ribs and from it he made a woman. She was named Eve.

God said to them, "You may eat freely from any tree of the garden, but if you eat from the tree of Knowledge of Good and Evil you will die."

God had created everything wonderful and perfect. It looked as if nothing could destroy the happiness. However, God's enemy, Satan, wished Adam and Eve would disobey God. In the form of a snake, Satan one day tempted and tricked Adam and Eve to eat of the forbidden fruit.

Immediately Adam and Eve felt bad and as a consequence, Adam and Eve could no longer live together with God.

It was a very sad day when they ate of the fruit. The paradise in the garden with God was lost for Adam and Eve. But it was not the end. God still loved His children, Adam and Eve. God did not forget them and He already had made a wonderful plan to get His children back.

# "Who told you that you are naked? Did you eat from the tree which I said you shall not eat?"

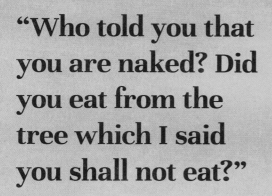

## Can you count the bees?

How many bees are flying around the bear in the picture below?

Answer: 16 bees

Can you find the bug?

# The Great Flood (Genesis 6-9)

The earth was full of people who were mean and cruel to one another. This made God very sad, but there was still one good man. His name was Noah. God said to Noah, "I am going to bring a massive flood on the earth to destroy it because I am sorry I have made it. I want to start all over again."

As Noah had found favor in the eyes of the Lord, God told him to build a giant ark. God told Noah and his sons exactly how to build the ark so that it could hold Noah's family and a one pair, a male and female, of all living animals in the world.

Noah and his sons spent many years building the ark. One day when it was finished God sent a pair of all animals to Noah. Two by two, the animals entered the ark. Storm clouds filled the sky. When Noah's family and all the animals entered the ark God shut the door. Then it started to rain. It rained and rained for forty days and nights. In the end even the mountaintops were under water. However, inside the ark, Noah, his family and all the animals were safe.

Finally, the rain stopped. God said, "Everybody can leave the ark now for the flooding is over!" Noah opened the door and all the animals rushed out into a fresh, new world. God set a rainbow in the sky. It was a sign of His promise to never again destroy the whole world with a flood.

"A pair of each animal that lives on dry land came to the ark and entered it."

# The Tower of Babel (Genesis 11)

A long time ago there was a big city full of many people. One day the people of the city said to each other, "Let's work together and build a tall tower that will reach up to heaven. That way we will be remembered and we will make a name for ourselves as the most important people on the earth."

God was not pleased and He knew what they were thinking. God did not want people to trust in themselves alone, instead He wanted them to trust in Him. God came down to look at the city and to see the tower that was being built.

God said, "If they can do this, there will be nothing that will be impossible for them." So, God disrupted their plans. He confused them by giving the people different languages. This meant that the workers could not understand each other. They were confused by the words the other builders used. This made them angry and frustated with each other and made it impossible for them to work together. In the end, the city with the great tower was never finished, because God confused the people.

# "If they can do this, there will be nothing that will be impossible for them."

## What is wrong?

Help the little bird find five differences between the two drawings.

Can you find the bird?

26

# A BIG
# TOWER

# God's Promise to Abraham

(Genesis 11-22)

There was a good man named Abraham. He was very wealthy and owned many cattle, sheep and camels. He also had a wife named Sarah. They both lived in a country far away in the East.

One day God said to Abraham, "Pack up all your things and leave your home country. I want you to go to the land that I will give to you. I promise I will bless you. Through you, all families of the earth will be blessed." Abraham obeyed and took Sarah and all their possessions and journeyed to the land of Canaan that God was going to give to them. Abraham was 75 years old. Sarah was 65. But they had no children. Abraham still believed that God would give them a family even though Sarah was old and unable to have children.

God knew Abraham was troubled. So, He came and spoke to him and said: "Look at the stars in the heavens. Count the stars if you can. That is how many descendants I will give you." Abraham trusted that God would keep His promise.

God kept his promise. Sarah became pregnant and gave birth to a son. She was 90 years old. Abraham was 100 when the baby boy was born. They named their son Isaac.

Can you find the turtle?

Color the stars to make them shine!

"Look at the stars in the heavens. Count the stars if you can."

# A Wife for Isaac (Genesis 24)

When Isaac grew up, Abraham wanted a good wife for him. One day Abraham called his oldest and most trusted servant to his tent and said, "Promise me that you will go back to my country and find a good wife for my son Isaac."

The servant took ten camels loaded with gifts and went on the journey. He made his camels stop to drink water by a well outside the city just as the women were coming out to draw water from it. He prayed, "O Lord, give me success and show kindness to my master Abraham. As I stand here by the well, I will say to the ladies, 'Please give me a drink from your jar.' Let the lady who says, 'Drink, and I will water your camels also' be the one You have chosen to be Isaac's wife."

As he was still praying, a young woman named Rebekah came out with a water jar. She was very beautiful. The servant said, "Please give me a little drink from your jar." Rebekah said, "Drink, my lord." Then she said, "I will also draw water for your camels until they have finished drinking." Again and again, she drew water from the well and emptied her jar, until all the camels were satisfied.

The servant watched Rebekah closely. Now he knew she would be a good wife for Isaac because God had chosen her. God had answered his prayer.

Can you find the snail?

# "Rebekah, may you become the mother of millions."

Color your own peacock!

# DRINK, MY LORD

# Joseph and the Dreams (Genesis 37, 39–41)

Joseph was the second youngest of Jacob's eleven sons. He was the favorite of his father, who loved him very much, and even had a beautiful and very expensive coat made for Joseph. When the brothers saw it they became very jealous and made an evil plan to get rid of Joseph. One day the brothers succeeded and sent him away to be a slave in Egypt. In Egypt, Joseph was blamed for something he did not do and sent to prison.

Joseph had many dreams and knew how to interpret them. Soon it was known in the prison that he understood what dreams meant. One day Pharaoh himself had a dream which worried him a lot.

36

"I was standing by the Nile River and saw seven fat, beautiful cows coming up out of the river to graze on the grass. Afterwards came seven skinny, ugly cows out of the river and then the skinny, ugly cows ate all the fat, beautiful cows."

Joseph was called to Pharaoh's palace from his prison cell to interpret the dream. He said, "The dream means this: first, Egypt will have seven good years with plenty of food to eat. Then there will be seven very bad years with no food at all."

Pharaoh said, "Since God has made this known to you, you shall be in charge of my palace. All people must obey your orders." In all Egypt, only Pharaoh was greater than Joseph.

38

"God will give you the answer to your dreams."

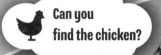

JOSEPH THE DREAMER

Can you find the chicken?

39

# The Baby in the Basket
(Exodus 1–2)

After many years, a new Pharaoh came to power. He decided did not like the Israelites, God's people and descendants of Abraham. He forced them to live as slaves in Egypt. They had to work hard and long and did not have much food. The evil Pharaoh was afraid that the Israelites would have so many children that they would outnumber the Egyptians and try to take over the kingdom. Therefore, he made a cruel and terrible decision that all the Israelites' baby boys should be killed. The Israelites were afraid and prayed to God for help.

One Israelite woman gave birth to a baby boy. She took care of him for three months but could not hide him from the soldiers any longer. She made a basket that could float like a boat. She then put the baby in it and sent the basket out on the river Nile. She trusted that God would save her baby. The little boy's sister, Miriam, hid and watched the basket float down the river.

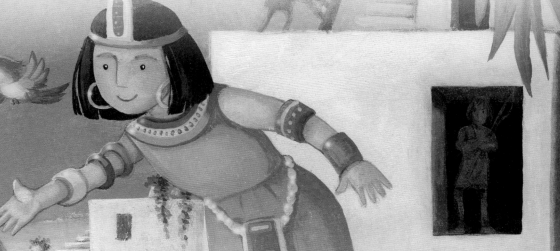

The daughter of Pharaoh came down to the river to bathe. The princess saw the basket floating among the reeds. She sent her servant to get it for her. When she opened it, the baby was crying. The princess was filled with compassion for the little baby boy.

Miriam boldly came up to the princess and asked, "Would you like me to find a woman who can nurse him for you?" The princess said, "Yes. Take this child into your house and care for him for me. I will pay you." Miriam was very happy when she took her brother back to his mother, who lovingly cared for him until he was old enough to eat food by himself. Then she brought him to the princess, who raised Moses in her palace.

Can you find the frog?

"I will name him Moses, because I have taken him out of the water."

GOD WILL HELP

# God Calls Moses (Exodus 3-4)

**M**oses was working as a shepherd out in a big desert when one day something very strange and amazing happened. He saw a bush on fire, but it did not burn up. Moses walked over to the bush. Just then God called him to from inside the burning bush.

God's voice came from the fire and said, "Do not come near. Take off your sandals. The place where you are standing is holy ground. I am the God of your father, the God of Abraham, the God of Isaac, and the God of Jacob." Moses hid his face because he was afraid to look at God.

God said to Moses, "Don't be afraid because I am with you. I have seen my people, the Israelites, suffering in Egypt and I have not forgotten them. Tell Pharaoh that the Israelites are my People and I want them to leave Egypt. Moses, you must lead them out of Egypt."

Moses was afraid to go back to Egypt and said, "Who am I to go to Pharaoh? And why would the People follow me?" God said to Moses, "Don't be afraid. I will be with you. Tell the children of Israel that I AM has sent you," Finally, Moses went to Egypt to tell Pharaoh to let the People go.

## What is wrong?

Help the rabbit find five differences between the two images.

# "I will keep you safe. Go now and I will be with you."

Can you find the bug?

I AM WHO I AM

47

# Through The Big Sea!

(Exodus 13-15)

After God sent ten plagues over Egypt, Pharaoh finally decided to let the People leave his kingdom. Moses led the Israelites on their journey. On their way they came to a big sea called the Red Sea, where they camped. Meanwhile, Pharaoh regretted his decision and sent out his big army to bring back the Israelites to Egypt.

When the Israelites saw the Egyptians approaching they were terrified. They said to Moses, "Why did you bring us out here in the desert to die?" Moses said, "Don't be afraid. Stand still and see how God will help us. God will fight for you. Just be still."

Then God sent a storm that blew so hard that the waters were pulled back. A wide path opened in the sea, right in front of the Israelites. The path led all the way to the other side of the sea. The Israelites could now escape from Pharaoh's army through the sea! They brought all their animals and belongings and did not even get wet.

Pharaoh saw that they were escaping and he gave orders for his men to follow them between the walls of water into the middle of the sea. Meanwhile, God told Moses to stretch out his hand. The waters rolled back and Pharaoh's army was destroyed. In this way, God saved His people and they no longer had to live as slaves in Egypt.

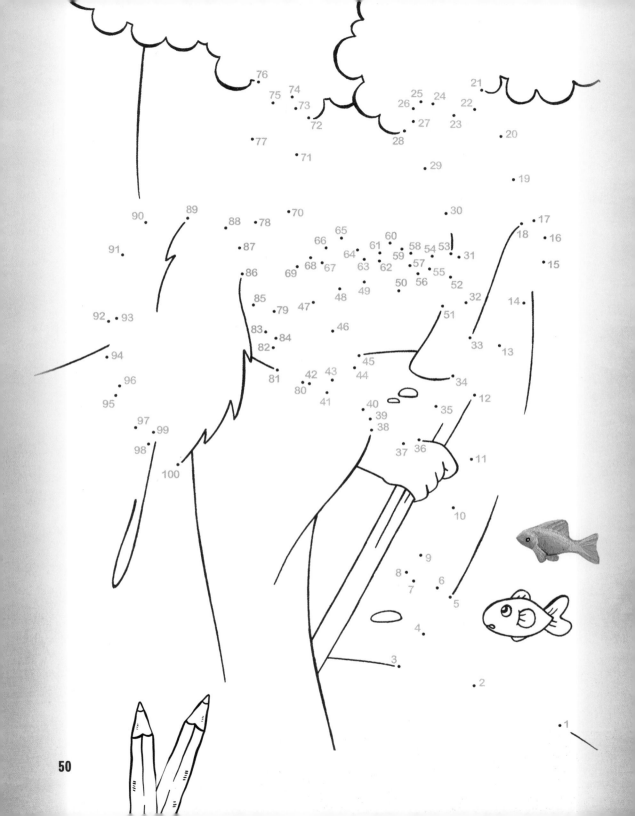

50

"Don't be afraid! God will fight for you."

# The Ten Commandments

(Exodus 19–34)

The Israelites continued their journey in the big desert. One day they arrived at the same mountain where Moses saw the burning bush. Moses climbed up the mountain to talk to God. For forty days, Moses stayed on the mountaintop as God talked to him. God gave Moses ten important commandments on two large, flat stones so that Moses could teach these instructions to God's people.

While Moses was away, the people gathered together and said to Moses' brother Aaron, "We don't know what has happened to Moses. Make some new gods for us so that we can worship them." Aaron told them to give him their gold earrings. He used a chisel to make a mold. He melted down the golden earrings and made a calf out of them. The people made burnt offerings to the golden calf, eating and drinking in celebration and worshipping it.

When Moses saw that people were worshipping a golden calf, he was very angry. He threw the tablets down to the ground, breaking them into pieces at the foot of the mountain. Moses said to Aaron, "What did these people do to you that made you lead them into something like this?" Moses then prayed to God for the people. Because Moses asked God to forgive them, God showed mercy and forgave the Israelites.

Can you find the rabbit?

"Worship God only, do not worship anything else."

GOD IS LOVE

# The Walls of Jericho

(Numbers 13-14, 27; Deuteronomy 34; Joshua 1-3, 5-6)

**M**oses was very old. Joshua was a brave and strong young man. Moses said, "Joshua, you must lead the people to their new home which God will give to them." They came to the city of Jericho. It had a thick mighty wall around it, with strong soldiers looking down from the walls. It was like a fortress.

Joshua was not worried, because God had already told him how the city could be defeated. Joshua commanded his army to march around the city every day for the next six days. Then, on the seventh day, God told the priests leading the army around the city walls to blow their trumpets, and all the people shouted out loud at the same time. All at once, the walls of Jericho came tumbling down. The Israelites easily captured the city.

Finally, after all these years in the desert, the Israelites were living in their own land. The promise so many years earlier to Abraham had been fulfilled by God.

### Can you count the stones?

How many stones are faling down?
Can you color the white ones?

Answer: 19 stones

"Shout! For the Lord has given you the city."

Can you find the dog?

59

# Samson (Judges 13-16)

Samson was a super strong, good leader in Israel. God said that from his birth to his death, he should never cut his hair as it was a sign that God was upon him. So he had long hair and a big flowing beard. Many times he fought Israel's enemies and helped God's people with his mighty powers. He was so strong he could kill even a lion with his bare hands.

One day the Philistines caught him. While he was sleeping, an evil woman had Samson's hair cut off. Immediately, Samson's strength left him. They tied him up and threw him in prison and blinded him by tearing out his eyes. However, Samson's hair began to grow again.

One day there was a party. The Philistines thought of making fun of Samson, so they brought him up from the prison. More than 3,000 people were gathered, and as they got more and more drunk, they also became more and more evil. Samson was standing between the pillars of the building, with a hand on each pillar.

Everybody had forgotten that much of Samson's hair had grown back while he was in prison. Samson prayed his last prayer to God and said, "God, please give me back my powers one last time." And God made him strong again. Samson pushed as hard as he could. The big pillars began to break and the roof came crashing down on all the people under it.

STRONG

Can you find the owl?

What color should the bear be?

"God, please give me back my powers one last time."

# David and Goliath (1 Samuel 17)

**D**avid was a shepherd and helped his father take care of his sheep. As David watched the sheep, he also became very skilled in using his sling. He learned how to throw stones at lions to protect the sheep. One day, his father asked him to bring lunch for his brothers, who were soldiers in the Israelite army.

The Philistines had gathered their armies for battle. In their army was a giant named Goliath, who was over nine feet tall. He bragged and made fun of God and the army of Israel and no one dared to stand up and fight him.

David said, "Don't be afraid! I will fight the giant!" Taking his shepherd's staff, David went by a small brook and chose five smooth stones. He put them in his pouch. With his sling in his hand, David approached Goliath. David then ran towards the giant while swinging his sling round and round. David sent off the stone and it hit Goliath right between his eyes. Goliath dropped to the ground.

Goliath was defeated. God had given David the strength to kill the giant and David gave God the glory for the victory. Many years later people made David, the shepherd boy, their new king. David was a great king who built a mighty kingdom and defeated Israel's many enemies.

# Jonah and the Fish (Jonah 1-4)

There was a man named Jonah and there was a city called Nineveh. God spoke to Jonah, "Go to the big city of Nineveh! The people there are doing bad things. Tell them to stop! I will forgive them." However, Jonah did not want to go to Nineveh because he did not like the people in there. Instead he went to the harbor and jumped on a boat that was going far away.

Jonah went down below deck to try and get some sleep. He wanted to escape from the job God had asked him to do. Meanwhile God sent a great storm. The storm was so mighty that the sailors on the boat thought the ship would fall apart. They were all very afraid and each one of them prayed to their own god.

"Oh, no!" said Jonah. "This is entirely my fault. I was not listening to what God told me to do. Please throw me into the sea." The sailors looked at each other and then they threw Jonah into the sea. By doing this the men on the boat were safe.

Jonah, on the other hand, was sinking deeper and deeper and deeper into the sea. Just when Jonah thought all was over, God sent a big fish to rescue him. It swallowed him with one big gulp. God had not forgotten Jonah. He made the fish spit Jonah up on a seashore three days later.

At that time Jonah was ready to listen to God. He went to Nineveh and people listened. God forgave them and the city was saved.

Can you find the shell?

"God had not forgotten Jonah."

PRAY TO GOD

70

# The Fiery Furnace (Daniel 1-3)

Shadrach, Meshach, and Abednego were good friends. They came from Israel as captives, to work in the house of King Nebuchadnezzar of Babylon. One day the king built a huge idol that was 90 feet tall, nine feet wide and covered with gold. He then sent out a message to the whole city that everyone must bow down and worship the king's wonderful golden statue. Anyone who would not bow down and worship the golden statue would be thrown into a burning, fiery furnace.

The three good friends did not want to pray to an idol and refused. They believed in the true living God, so they did not want to bow down to the golden statue. When the king heard about it he was so furious that he ordered the furnace to be heated seven times hotter than usual. He then ordered his soldiers to throw the men headfirst into the burning, fiery furnace.

However, an amazing thing happened. The fire did not hurt the three friends. It did not even burn their clothes and they began walking around inside the furnace. The three friends were not alone in the furnace as God had sent an angel to rescue them.

The King went to the furnace and called, "Shadrach, Meshach, and Abednego, servants of the Most High God, come out of the fire!" Calmly, the three friends walked out of the furnace. They did not even smell burnt from the fires they had been in. King Nebuchadnezzar knew that God had saved them and realized the power of God.

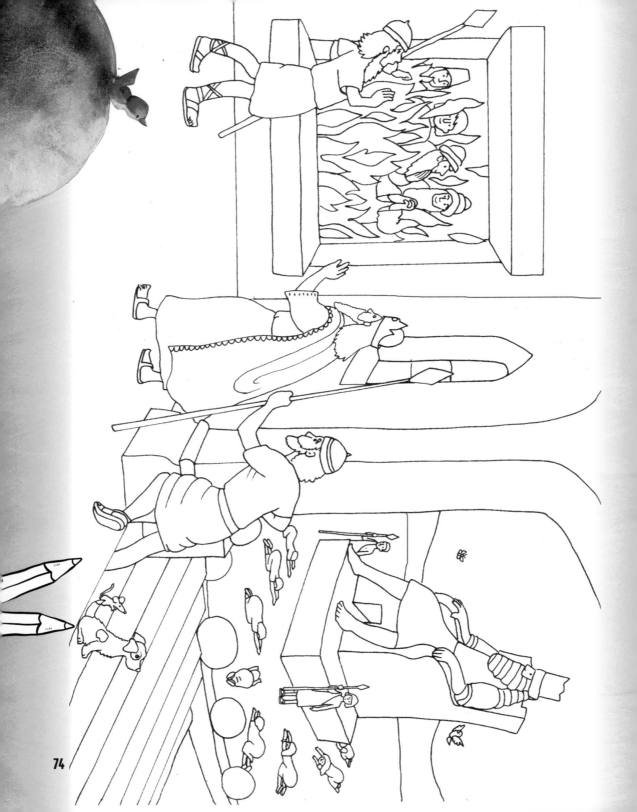

# Daniel and the Lions (Daniel 6)

**D**aniel also worked for the king of Babylon. The king liked Daniel very much and said, "No one works as hard and well as Daniel. I want him to have the best job in my kingdom." This made the king's other servants very angry and jealous, and they decided to set up a trap for Daniel.

Daniel loved God very much and he prayed to God three times a day. This gave the evil servants an idea. They went to the king and said, "We think there should be a new law: no one can pray to anyone else than the king." The king liked the plan and made this a new law.

Daniel kept on praying to God. Daniel knew the men were watching him but he was not afraid and knew it was more important to pray to God than follow the new law the king had made. Soon the King heard that Daniel was praying to God. He was very sad because he liked Daniel but also knew that he had to uphold his own new law. So the king sent out his soldiers to arrest Daniel. As punishment, they threw him into a lions' den filed with scary lions.

Early in the morning, as soon as the sun came up, the king rushed out to the lions' den and called, "Daniel! Daniel! Are you there?" "Yes," Daniel said. "God sent an angel and the lions did not harm me." The king was very happy and ordered Daniel to be pulled up from the den. He then said, "Daniel's God is the best and true God in the world. Pray to Him instead – not to me."

Can you find the spider?

# "God sent His angel to shut the mouths of the lions."

What color should the lion be?

# The New Testament

# The Birth of Jesus

(Luke 1-2, Matthew 1)

A little over two thousand years ago there was a young woman named Mary. She loved God and had promised to marry a man named Joseph. One day when Mary was at home, suddenly, God's angel Gabriel stood before her and said, "Mary, do not be afraid. You are the most blessed woman as God wants to bring His Son into the world through you. You will become pregnant by the Holy Spirit and you shall name the boy Jesus."

It went just as the angel had told, and nine months later Mary was almost ready to have her baby. At that time they had to travel to Bethlehem by order of the ruler of the country. When they arrived in Bethlehem, every room was full. However, there was a stable where they could stay. In the silent night, Mary gave birth to Jesus.

In the same area that night, shepherds were in the fields taking care of their sheep. Suddenly, a shining angel appeared and said to them, "Do not be afraid. I bring you the greatest news. God's own Son has been born this night in Bethlehem. You will find him sleeping in a stable. Find him and worship him!" The shepherds hurried to town, found the stable, and entered. When they saw baby Jesus they praised God and worshipped Jesus as their Savior.

EMMANUEL

"Glory to God in the highest! May God give peace on earth to men with whom He is pleased!"

Can you find the owl?

# Jesus' Baptism (Matthew 3; Mark 1, John 1)

When Jesus was around thirty years old, he started speaking to people about God. At the same time there was a man who lived far from town near the Jordan River. People called him John the Baptist or John the Baptizer. Actually, he was Jesus' cousin. "Turn to God! Get ready! God's messenger will be here soon," John shouted.

One day Jesus came to see John as he was baptizing people at the Jordan River. Jesus went over and asked to be baptized by John. When he came up from the water, something amazing happened. The voice of God was heard from the sky saying, "This is My Son. I love Him. Listen to Him!" At the same time it looked as if a white dove was descending down from heaven upon Jesus. This was God's Holy Spirit. Now Jesus was ready to begin his work.

Can you find the frog?

**"This is My Son. I love Him very much."**

How do you want to color the pelicans?

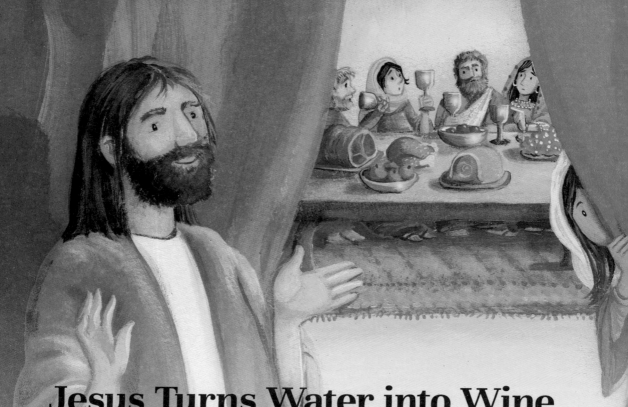

# Jesus Turns Water into Wine
(John 2)

Jesus and some of his disciples were invited to a big wedding in Cana. Jesus' mother, Mary, was also invited. They were served the most wonderful food and wine. During the party, Mary came to Jesus and brought bad news, "I found out that the wine is all gone. They don't have more to serve. Can you help them?"

Mary then said to the servants, "Do whatever He tells you to do!" There were six large stone jars. Jesus told the servants, "Fill the jars with water." The servants filled them to the very top. Then Jesus said, "Take some out and give it to the man in charge of the feast." So they took it to him.

The manager of the feast took a drink. It wasn't water anymore. Jesus used His power to make the water change into the most fantastic wine. God had given Jesus the power to change water into wine. It was a miracle, which is a special sign from God showing His power. This was only the first of many miracles Jesus did.

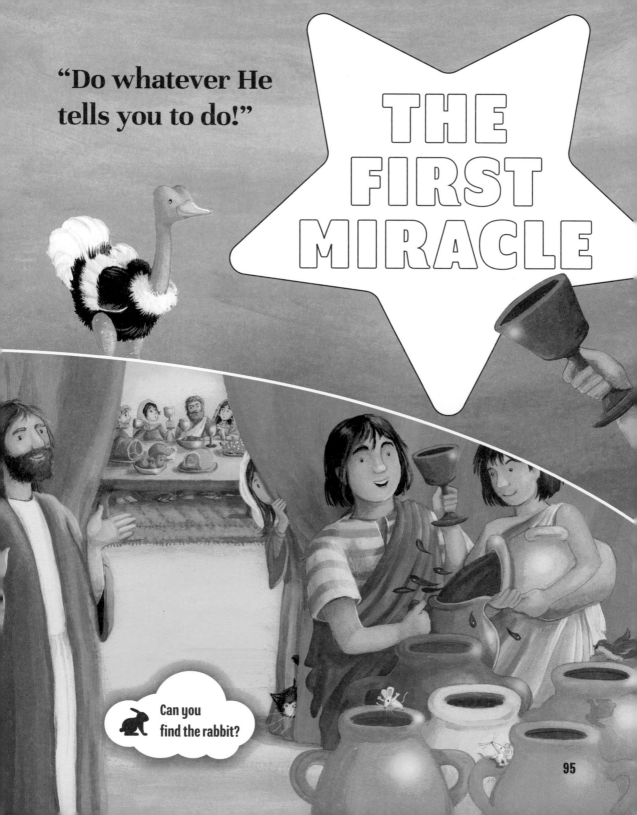

# The Stilling of the Storm

(Luke 8:22-25)

It was a late evening and Jesus had been teaching people all day about God's love. Jesus said to His disciples, "Let's cross to the other side of the lake."

Jesus was tired. As they sailed, He fell asleep in the back of the boat. Suddenly, a very bad storm came up on the lake. The waves were coming over the sides and into the boat, and it was almost full of water. Jesus was still sleeping calmly. The disciples woke him up and said, "Jesus, don't you care about us? We are going to drown!"

Jesus got up. He said to the disciples, "Why are you afraid? Your faith is so weak." He harshly scolded the wind, "Hush!" He said to the sea, "Peace. Be still!" Immediately the wind stopped blowing and it was completely calm.

The disciples were amazed and said to each other, "Who is this? He commands the wind and the sea and they obey Him!"

BE STILL!

Can you find the fish?

"Who is this? He commands the wind and the sea and they obey Him!"

Color the boat in your favorite colors!

# Jesus Feeds Thousands

(Matthew 14, Mark 6, Luke 9)

Once there were more than 5,000 people who followed Jesus to a place far away from any town. It was getting late and Jesus could see that everyone was very hungry. But there was no food. However, there was a little boy, whom the disciples took to Jesus. He had brought two fish and five loaves of bread with him. Jesus said, "Just bring me what you have. This will do!"

So the little boy gave Jesus his lunch and waited excitedly to see what would happen with his food. Jesus thanked God for the food and started breaking pieces off the bread and fish. No matter how much they broke from the bread and fish, there was always something left.

When everybody was full, the disciples gathered twelve baskets of the leftovers. In Jesus' hands, the little boy's five loaves of bread and two fish fed more than 5,000 people on that day. It was truly a miracle.

# "Give them something to eat!"

Can you find the snail?

102

# The Good Samaritan (Luke 10)

**P**eople loved to hear what Jesus could tell about God. Everybody loved to be near him and listen to his words. One day Jesus told a very important story.

It was the story of a man travelling from Jerusalem to Jericho. Some robbers beat him up and left him beside the road to die. Soon, a priest from the temple in Jerusalem came by. He saw the poor, hurt man but looked the other way and walked on without helping.

Not long after came another man who worked in the temple. He also saw the man, but just like the priest, he passed by, looking the other way without stopping to help. Now a good man from Samaria came down the road. Jews and people from Samaria never got along and always tried to avoid each other. But the good Samaritan felt sorry for the man who was hurt. He stopped and got off his donkey. The Samaritan bandaged the man's wounds and took him to an inn. He promised to pay whatever it would cost for the man to get well again.

Jesus then said, "In the same way you should also be kind to everyone you meet."

Can you find the bird?

"Be kind to anyone you meet."

A GOOD FRIEND

# The Good Shepherd

(Luke 15, John 10:1-18)

Jesus told many stories and people loved to hear them because they were really about God. Jesus told stories about finding a lost sheep, a missing coin, and a story about a father and his sons.

Jesus said, "A shepherd had one hundred sheep. Every evening when they returned home, the shepherd carefully counted all his sheep before he locked them behind the fence so they were safe from the wild animals for the night. One evening, as the shepherd returned back home, he only counted 99 sheep and knew a sheep had wandered away somewhere.

It was getting very dark, but the shepherd knew that he had to leave the 99 sheep inside the fence and go out to find the missing sheep. The shepherd went out searching in the dark fields. The sun was almost below the horizon, but he went further and further away from home to find the sheep. Suddenly, he heard the sheep calling and rushed to find it. He found the sheep, took it and placed it on the back of his shoulders and carried it back home.

Jesus then said, "God is like this good shepherd. If someone is lost, God will search and search, find and bring him back home again. But God's love and joy is so much bigger than the shepherd's, because people are so much more valuable to God than sheep are."

Can you find the bug?

"I am the good shepherd. The good shepherd lays down his life for the sheep."

## What is wrong?

Help the little bird to find five differences between the two drawings.

# Jesus Loves Children

(Matthew 18-19, Mark 9-10, Luke 18)

Jesus loved children and showed His special care for them many times. Some people brought little children and babies to Jesus to have Him touch them and pray for them. But Jesus' disciples tried to keep the children away from Him because they thought Jesus was too busy with more important things to spend time with small children.

When Jesus heard that the disciples were trying to send the children away he was very upset. He said, "No! You must let these little children come to Me. I tell you this: If you are not going to be like these small children, you will never understand God's Kingdom. Let the little children come to Me, for they really belong to God."

Jesus then took the children in His arms. He laid his hands on them and He blessed them.

# JESUS LOVES YOU

Can you find the chicken?

"Let the little children come to Me, for they really belong to God."

Decorate the hearts in different patterns and colors!

# Lazarus, Wake Up! (Luke 11)

**J**esus often visited two sisters living in a town called Bethany. Their names were Martha and Mary. They also had a brother named Lazarus. One day, Lazarus became very sick and died.

When Jesus heard that his good friend Lazarus was dead, he said, "Our friend Lazarus has fallen asleep. I will go and wake him up." Some days later, when Jesus came to Bethany, Lazarus' body had been in a tomb for four days. Mary was crying and very sad. But Jesus said to Mary, "Your brother will rise again."

Jesus went over to the tomb. It was a cave with a big rock rolled in front of the entrance. Jesus said, "Roll the stone away!" When they took the stone away, Jesus looked up and said, "Father, thank You for listening. I know that You always hear Me." Jesus then called in a loud voice, "Lazarus, come out!"

When Jesus said this, Lazarus, who had been dead, walked out, alive and perfectly healthy. His feet and hands were still wrapped in linen strips. A large cloth covered his face. Jesus said, "Unwrap him. Let him go." All who saw this were completely astonished to see that God had given Jesus the power to raise Lazarus from the dead.

"I am the resurrection and the life. Everyone who believes in Me, even if he dies, will live."

Can you find the turtle?

Can you draw stripes on the zebra?

118

# The Last Days of Jesus in Jerusalem (Matthew 21, Mark 11, Luke 19, John 12)

Jesus knew the time had come to finish God's plan to be our Savior. He traveled to Jerusalem to celebrate Passover with His disciples. Jesus, knowing all that would happen to Him, sent two of His disciples with these instructions: "Go into the village. When you enter it, you will find a donkey, and a colt that has never been ridden. Untie them and bring them to Me. If anyone asks you why you are untying them, say, 'The Lord needs them and will send them back immediately after.'"

The disciples went and found the animals just as the Lord told them. As they were untying the donkey and colt, the owners said to them, "Why are you untying our colt and donkey?" They replied, "The Lord needs them," and the owners let them take the animals.

The disciples put their coats on the back of the colt. Jesus sat down on the coats and they entered Jerusalem. Word spread quickly that Jesus had come to Jerusalem and people ran from everywhere to see Him. Many of the people laid their cloaks upon the road. Others cut down palm branches and leafy branches from the fields to spread them on the path. They celebrated Jesus' coming, hoping He would be their new king and throw out the Roman soldiers. They shouted, "Blessed is He who comes in the name of the Lord! Hosanna in the highest!" But Jesus was not that kind of king.

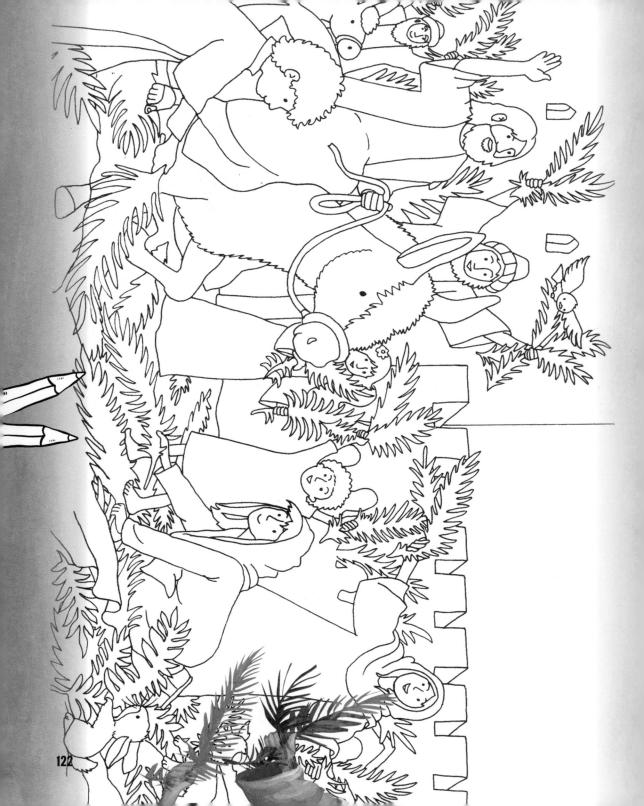

# HOSANNA! HOSANNA!

## "The Lord needs them."

# When Jesus Died

(Matthew 26-27, Mark 14-15, Luke 22-23, John 13-19)

Jesus and the disciples gathered to share the Passover meal. Jesus shared wine and bread with them. He told the disciples to remember him in this way after he leaves them. Jesus knew it was nearly time for him to leave the world and go back to God.

Later that evening, soldiers found Jesus and arrested him. They took Jesus to the Roman governor Pilate who questioned him based on many false accusations. Meanwhile more and more people gathered. They all shouted, "Crucify Jesus. We want him dead!"

The next day the soldiers took Jesus to a place called Golgotha. They nailed him to a cross. "Father, forgive them. They don't know what they are doing," Jesus gasped. Upon the place came a great darkness. Jesus shouted, "Father, I give you my life! It is finished!" and then he died. He had done it. Jesus had sacrificed himself and rescued the whole world.

Can you find the mouse?

"It is Finished!"

I.N.R.I

127

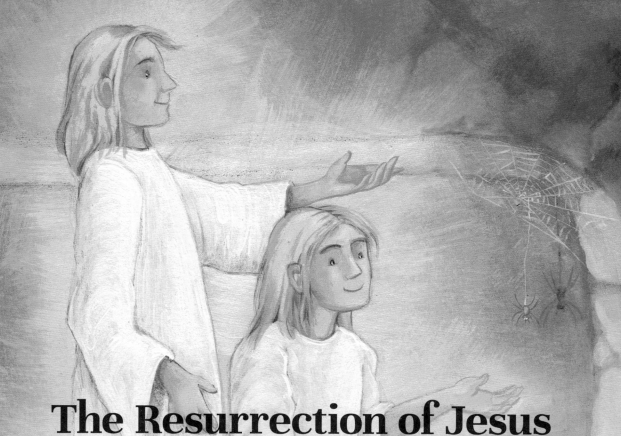

# The Resurrection of Jesus

(Matthew 28, Mark 16, Luke 24, John 20, 1 Peter 3)

Early in the morning, on the third day, after Jesus' death the two disciples Peter and John, and a woman named Mary Magdalene, came to see the cave where Jesus was buried. When they came near to the tomb, they could see that the big stone had been rolled away. Jesus was no longer there. The grave was empty.

.Peter went inside the cave and found cloth that had been wrapped around Jesus' body. The piece of cloth that had been wrapped around Jesus' head was neatly folded beside it. Mary Magdalene also entered the cave. She saw two angels. One of them said to her, "Why are you

looking for Jesus here? Jesus has risen from the dead and is alive again just like He told you."

Mary came out of the cave. When she turned around, she saw Jesus standing there, but she did not know who He was. Jesus asked her, "Why are you crying?" Mary thought He was the gardener and said, "Sir, if you have taken His body away, please, tell me." Then Jesus said to her, "Mary". Finally, Mary realized Jesus was standing right beside her and that He was alive again. She hugged Him tightly. Then she went back to tell everybody the wonderful news.

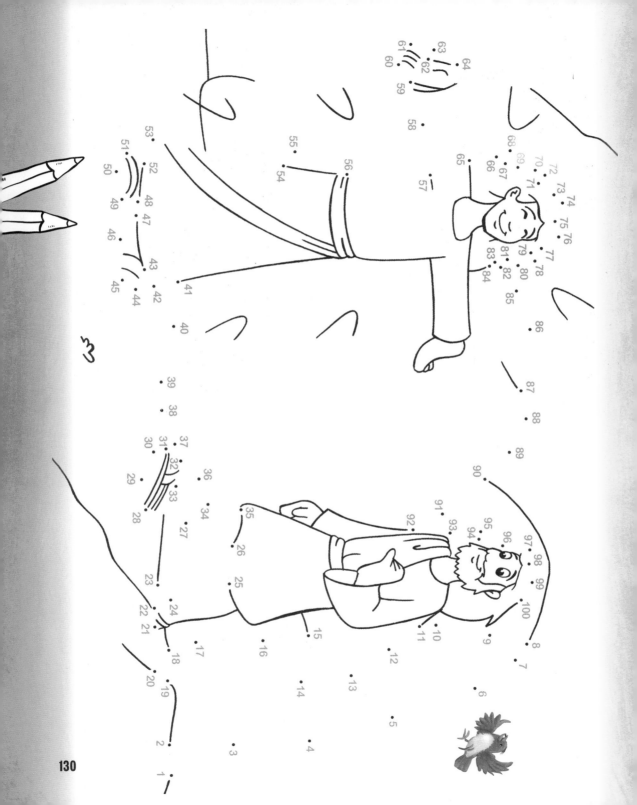

130

Can you find the spider?

"Jesus is no longer here. He has risen from the dead and is alive again just like He told you."

THE TOMB IS EMPTY

# Jesus Returns to Heaven

(Luke 24, Acts 1)

Jesus appeared to all his friends and the disciples. They were full of joy to see Jesus alive again. Later on, Jesus even appeared to more than 500 people gathered together. Jesus told His disciples, "Go and make more disciples of people everywhere. Baptize them in the name of the Father and of the Son and of the Holy Spirit. Teach them to do all that I have taught you! I will be with you always to the end of time."

Jesus knew it was time for Him to return to heaven. So, Jesus took his disciples to a hill outside of Jerusalem. Jesus said, "It's time for me to go back to heaven to be with my Father. After I'm back in heaven, you must go back to Jerusalem and wait there until I will send My Spirit to you. After that, you will go to every part of the world to tell people about Me and everything I taught you when we were together."

As He was talking to them, Jesus began to rise up to Heaven. The disciples stared, looking up, as Jesus went higher and higher into the sky. Then a cloud hid Him from their sight. Suddenly two men dressed in white shining clothes stood right next to them. They were angels and asked, "Why are you standing here looking at the sky? Jesus has gone to heaven and one day Jesus will come back to Earth again the same way you have now seen Him leave earth." The disciples knelt and worshiped Jesus and they then returned to Jerusalem with a happy heart.

Can you find the cat?

"I will be with you always to the end of time."

ONE DAY JESUS WILL RETURN

# God's Wonderful City – Our True Home!

(Revelation 4, 21-22)

The Bible tells us that when Jesus returns, there will be a new heaven and a new earth. On this new earth, there will not be any sickness or death. There will be a big beautiful city with streets of polished gold and buildings made of shimmering gold and glass. In the middle of the city there is a beautiful river, with trees on both sides. The most wonderful fruits grow on these trees every month, and the leaves can heal people.

It will never be night in Heaven. God's children will not need a light or the sun because God Himself will be the light and shine on us. Only good and wonderful things happen there. The most wonderful and amazing thing about it is that God our Father and Jesus will live there with us forever. Jesus is waiting for us to be there with Him when we leave this world. He is preparing a home for us, and there is plenty of room for everyone.

# HEAVEN IS

# "Jesus is preparing a home for us, and there is plenty of room for everyone."

What color should the sheep be?

# The Lord's Prayer

Our Father in heaven,
hallowed be Your name.
Your Kingdom come,
Your will be done
on earth as in heaven.
Give us today our daily bread.
Forgive us our sins
as we forgive those who sin against us.
Lead us not into temptation,
but deliver us from evil.
For the kingdom,
the power and the glory are Yours
now and forever.
Amen.

(Matthew 6, Luke 11)

# WRITE YOUR OWN PRAYER